GREAT MINDS OF SCIENCE

CHARLES DARWIN

Groundbreaking Naturalist and Evolutionary Theorist

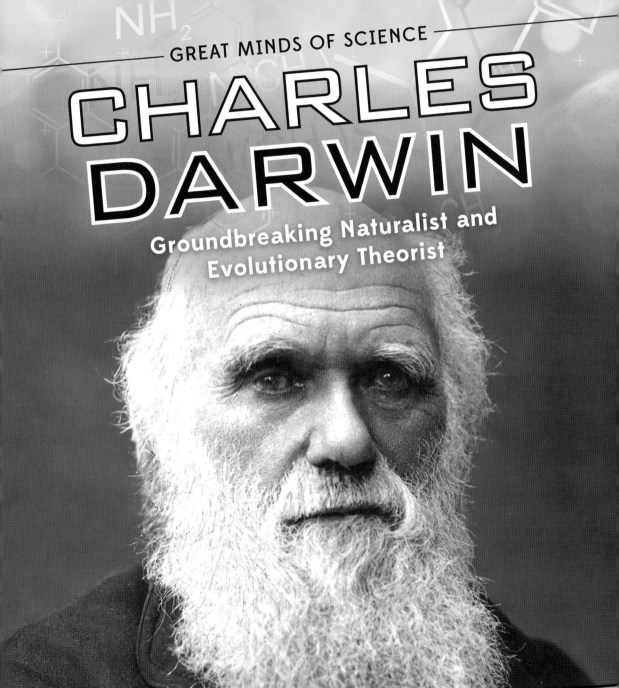

by Laura L. Sullivan

Content Consultant
Stephen C. Burnett, PhD
Professor of Biology
Clayton State University

Core Library

An Imprint of Abdo Publishing
abdopublishing.com

abdopublishing.com

Printed in the United States of America, North Mankato, Minnesota
032015
092015

THIS BOOK CONTAINS
RECYCLED MATERIALS

Cover Photo: Agencia el Universal/GDA/El Universal/México/AP Images
Interior Photos: Agencia el Universal/GDA/El Universal/México/AP Images, 1; Pictore/iStockphoto, 4; Ellen Sharples, 6; Henrik Larsson/Shutterstock Images, 8; Shutterstock Images, 10, 19; George Richmond, 12, 25; Friedrich George Weitsch, 15; R.T. Pritchett, 17; Ryan M. Bolton/Shutterstock Images, 18, 45; Messrs. Maull and Fox, 20; John Gould, 23; Public Domain, 27; iStockphoto, 29; John Collier, 32, 43; Bettmann/Corbis, 37; Ed Stock/iStockphoto, 39

Editor: Jenna Gleisner
Series Designer: Becky Daum

Library of Congress Control Number: 2015931127

Cataloging-in-Publication Data
Sullivan, Laura L.
 Charles Darwin: Groundbreaking naturalist and evolutionary theorist / Laura L. Sullivan.
   p. cm. -- (Great minds of science)
Includes bibliographical references and index.
ISBN 978-1-62403-872-3
1. Darwin, Charles, 1809-1882--Juvenile literature. 2. Naturalists--England--Biography--Juvenile literature. 3. Evolution (Biology)--Juvenile literature. I. Title.
576.8/2092--dc23
   [B]   2015931127

CONTENTS

A SCIENTIST IS BORN

On February 12, 1809, Charles Darwin was born in Shropshire, England, near the Welsh border. His mother was often ill. She died when Charles was only eight years old. Young Charles was then raised by his father and three older sisters. Charles's family members were freethinkers, and he was too. They believed reason, logic, and science were more important than tradition

Charles Darwin became known as a famous scientist later in life.

Charles Darwin studied the world and all living things from an early age.

or religion. Charles was surrounded and influenced by people who questioned and explored the world around them. He became one of the world's most accomplished naturalists—someone who studies animals and plants in their natural environment.

From his earliest years, Charles loved being outdoors. He enjoyed collecting items from nature. He brought home shells, insects, plants, and rocks. Then he tried to identify them. He watched birds and even collected bird eggs. He was careful to never take more than one egg from a nest. Young Charles also enjoyed swimming, hunting, and fishing.

School Days

As a child, Charles disliked school. He felt teachers taught the same topics over and over again. He also wanted more time to discover things on his own. In the early 1800s, schools focused on teaching Latin and Greek. Charles was not good at learning languages.

Education in Darwin's Day

For much of the 1800s, upper-class English children mainly studied Latin and Greek. They rarely learned other topics. Over time schools began teaching mathematics, science, history, geography, and literature. England's Grammar School Act of 1840 made sure literature and science, as well as Latin and Greek, were taught in every school.

Darwin once caught a rare crucifix beetle but lost it while trying to handle three different beetles.

Because of this, most of his teachers described him as an average student.

Charles's father was a doctor. He hoped his son would become one too. In October 1825, at age 16, Charles went to medical school at Edinburgh University. He did not like it. He found the lectures dull and thought the professors' facts were outdated. Charles also hated the sight of blood. One time he saw a child being operated on and had to run out of the room. Not long after, he left medical school.

In 1827 Charles went to the University of Cambridge. While there, he studied Greek, Latin, and mathematics. Charles often did not do his schoolwork. Instead he studied nature and took part in long debates with his classmates. In his free time, Charles became an avid botanist, or a person who studies plants. He also collected beetles.

In January 1831 Charles passed his final exams. Now his father wanted him to become

Darwin's Beetles

Darwin collected plants and rocks. But he also collected beetles while at Cambridge. One day he pulled back some tree bark and found two rare beetles. He caught one in his left hand and the other in his right. Then he saw an even rarer beetle, called the crucifix ground beetle. He was eager to catch it but did not have a free hand. He popped one of the other beetles in his mouth and reached for the new one. The beetle squirted a nasty liquid in his mouth, causing him to spit it out and lose it. He also lost the rare crucifix beetle.

Darwin attended Christ's College at the University of Cambridge.

a priest. But Charles had other ideas for his future. Charles did not have to work to pay bills like most young men his age. Charles's parents gave him enough money to pay for a good education and study science. His parents' wealth also allowed him to travel the world.

FURTHER EVIDENCE

Chapter One shows how Charles Darwin's interests as a child led to his career as a naturalist. Visit the website below to read about Darwin's life in his own words. Find three quotes that support the idea that his childhood influenced his future career choice. Now look for information about his childhood that might have led him away from becoming a naturalist. Do you think Darwin's family life influenced his career choice? Why or why not?

Darwin's Early School Years
mycorelibrary.com/charles-darwin

ABOARD THE *BEAGLE*

While he was at Cambridge, Darwin was inspired by the writings of the naturalist and explorer Alexander von Humboldt. Humboldt spent many years studying plants and animals in Latin America. Darwin once described Humboldt as "the greatest scientific traveler who ever lived." Darwin was determined to follow in Humboldt's footsteps. Shortly after he

As a young man, Darwin agreed to embark on a journey that would change his life.

graduated college, Darwin hoped to sail to the tropics.

A friend told Darwin that Captain Robert FitzRoy was seeking a naturalist to go on his next voyage.

Alexander von Humboldt

Alexander von Humboldt (1769–1859) was a famous explorer and naturalist. Darwin was inspired by his work. He read Humboldt's travel books while in college. Darwin even visited some of the same places in Latin America that Humboldt explored. Humboldt has many plants and animals named after him, including the Humboldt squid and the Humboldt penguin. Some were named after him because he discovered them. Others were named in his honor.

Captain FitzRoy's main mission was to chart South America's coastline. Darwin jumped at the chance. But his father forbade him from going. He thought it was a crazy idea. He said if Darwin could find one person of common sense to approve of the scheme, he would allow it. Darwin's uncle, Josiah Wedgwood, supported the idea. He convinced Darwin's father to let Darwin go.

Darwin aspired to explore and follow in the footsteps of famous naturalist Alexander von Humboldt.

A Voyage of Discovery

On December 27, 1831, Darwin boarded FitzRoy's ship, the HMS *Beagle*. At each stop along South America's coast, Darwin studied the geology and animal life. Sometimes he wrote notes, drew sketches, or dissected specimens. Other times he packed specimens up to send back to England to be studied by experts.

The HMS *Beagle* took Darwin along the coast of South America and to many islands, such as the Galapagos Islands. Darwin loved exploring the tropical jungles. He made long journeys inland. Sometimes the

Darwin the Geologist

Darwin did not study only plants and animals. He was also interested in geology, or the study of rocks, minerals, and the history of Earth. While in Chile, Darwin survived an earthquake. He later found that the earthquake had exposed ancient mussel beds high above sea level. Mussels are marine animals. Darwin realized this part of Earth must have been underwater and risen over time. He also realized islands could sometimes sink beneath the sea.

Darwin was aboard the HMS *Beagle* for five years as the ship and its crew traveled around South America.

HMS *Beagle* waited for him. Other times he arranged to meet it at another coastal city.

Darwin found many fossils on his voyage. He began forming theories about how different extinct species related to one another. He could see some similarities between living and extinct animals. He also saw many differences. He began to wonder how the changes came about.

One of Darwin's most important discoveries was that each finch species had a different-shaped beak.

While visiting the Galapagos Islands, Darwin found that each island had its own variety of finch species. Each species was suited to the food available on each island. Some finches had heavy, strong beaks. These beaks were effective for cracking open seeds. Other finches had beaks that were suited for grasping or probing, which helped them catch insects. Darwin

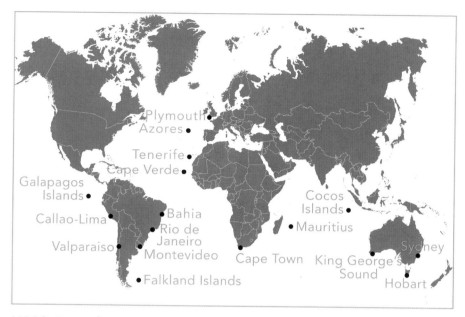

HMS *Beagle* Voyage

This map shows all the places Darwin visited on his voyage with the HMS *Beagle*. Which parts of the globe did he visit? Which continents or places did he not visit? How does this map help you better visualize the travels Darwin took while aboard the HMS *Beagle*?

collected the birds. But he did not study them at the time. Instead he preserved them for a specialist to study later.

CHAPTER THREE

A BOLD NEW IDEA

The HMS *Beagle* returned to England on October 2, 1836. Even before returning, Darwin was becoming famous. People were excited about the many specimens he had collected and sent home to England. When Darwin came home, he began writing. One of his books, *Zoology of the Voyage of the HMS Beagle*, included experts' descriptions of all the animal life he sent back

After returning home from his voyage, Darwin went to work on his new ideas.

to England. Even more popular was Darwin's journal of his trip, titled *The Voyage of the Beagle*. Alexander Humboldt wrote to Darwin, telling him what a good book it was.

After returning, Darwin learned he had made a mistake with his Galapagos Islands finches. He had not separated them according to the islands they came from. Instead he had placed them all in one bag. In 1837 scientist John Gould began to classify the birds. He told Darwin the finches' beaks were suited to different foods. Darwin began to think maybe one type of bird from the mainland had somehow changed to suit the food it found on each of the islands. If so, that one type of bird had become all of the different species of birds found on the Galapagos Islands.

Theory of Evolution by Natural Selection

On September 28, 1838, Darwin wrote a new idea in his notebook. He believed too many animals are

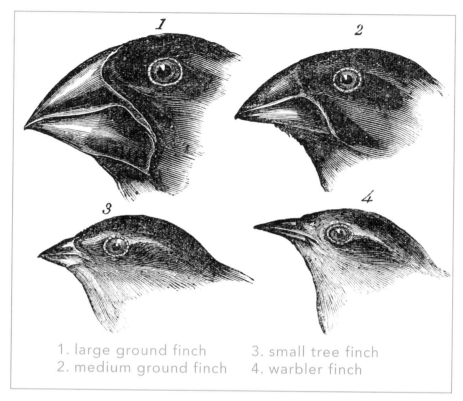

1. large ground finch   3. small tree finch
2. medium ground finch   4. warbler finch

Darwin's Finches

This diagram shows how the finches of the Galapagos Islands adapted to different diets. Look at their beaks. Finches one and two are both seedeaters, while finches three and four are insect eaters. What differences do you notice in the beaks? How do you think each beak helped each finch eat its particular source of food?

born. He noted every animal struggles to live. Only the ones most suited to their environment survive. The ones that survive reproduce, so their strong traits are passed on. He called this idea natural selection. Darwin knew humans could breed animals for certain

Another Theory of Evolution

Before Darwin's theory of evolution through natural selection, there was another popular idea about how different species came to be. Scientist Jean-Baptiste Lamarck (1744–1829) thought animals could inherit certain traits from their parents. If a mother giraffe stretched her neck to reach the highest tree branches, her children would be born with longer necks, for example. Even before Lamarck and Darwin's ideas of evolution, many scientists questioned changes in animal species. Some theories of evolution date back to ancient Greece, Rome, China, and other cultures.

traits through a process called artificial selection. He decided this process must happen in nature as well, most likely over long periods of time. He thought about this idea for many years before he told anyone about it.

Darwin married his cousin, Emma Wedgwood, in 1839. Soon after, he bought a house and 20 acres (8 ha) in the village of Downe, near Kent. It was around this time Darwin started to believe species were not made by a god or creator. He began to think species

abdopublishing.com

Published by Abdo Publishing, a division of ABDO, PO Box 398166,
Minneapolis, Minnesota 55439. Copyright © 2016 by Abdo Consulting
Group, Inc. International copyrights reserved in all countries. No part of
this book may be reproduced in any form without written permission from
the publisher. Core Library™ is a trademark and logo of Abdo Publishing.

Printed in the United States of America, North Mankato, Minnesota
032015
092015

Cover Photo: Agencia el Universal/GDA/El Universal/México/AP Images
Interior Photos: Agencia el Universal/GDA/El Universal/México/AP
Images, 1; Pictore/iStockphoto, 4; Ellen Sharples, 6; Henrik Larsson/
Shutterstock Images, 8; Shutterstock Images, 10, 19; George Richmond,
12, 25; Friedrich George Weitsch, 15; R.T. Pritchett, 17; Ryan M. Bolton/
Shutterstock Images, 18, 45; Messrs. Maull and Fox, 20; John Gould, 23;
Public Domain, 27; iStockphoto, 29; John Collier, 32, 43; Bettmann/Corbis,
37; Ed Stock/iStockphoto, 39

Editor: Jenna Gleisner
Series Designer: Becky Daum

Library of Congress Control Number: 2015931127

Cataloging-in-Publication Data
Sullivan, Laura L.
 Charles Darwin: Groundbreaking naturalist and evolutionary theorist /
Laura L. Sullivan.
   p. cm. -- (Great minds of science)
Includes bibliographical references and index.
ISBN 978-1-62403-872-3
1. Darwin, Charles, 1809-1882--Juvenile literature. 2. Naturalists--England-
-Biography--Juvenile literature. 3. Evolution (Biology)--Juvenile literature.
I. Title.
576.8/2092--dc23
[B]   2015931127